Three Years in the
Rocky Mountains

by
David L. Brown

Originally published
September 8-13, 1845
in
Cincinnati Daily Morning Atlas

Three Years in the Rocky Mountains

Finding my constitution debilitated by a residence of five years in some of the most unhealthy districts of Louisiana and Mississippi, and thinking that a change of climate, as well as habits and modes of life, might prove beneficial, I resolved in the spring of 1836, to take a trip to the far-off regions of the Rocky Mountains.

All preliminaries having been adjusted in a satisfactory manner, I embarked at St. Louis, on board the steamboat St. Peters, bound for the town of Independence. She was laden principally with an equipment of goods destined for the supply of the trappers and hunters in the employment of the North American Fur Company, in the perilous pursuit of beaver and otter, in the distant solitudes surrounding the sources of the Columbia, the Missouri, and the Platte. I ought likewise to state that besides the merchandise already mentioned there were some sixty or seventy daring and hirsute men, whose special business it was to protect this property in its tedious and somewhat dangerous transit across the almost interminable prairies that intervene between the outskirts of the United States territories, at times infested with hostile Indians, and the distant scenes of trapping and hunting. Nothing of any importance occurred in the upward passage; and in the course of five or six days, we found ourselves occupying a temporary rendezvous on the waters of the Kansas river, some thirty miles to the East of Canton Leavenworth. Here we remained for two or three weeks, in order to give our horses and mules a chance to get into tolerable condition, and likewise to allow the season to advance sufficiently far to have good grass on the journey.

Here we were joined by Captain Stewart, of the British army, Mr. Miller, (an artist) and a Mr. Phillipson, both of whom were in the Captain's suite, as likewise an Indian half-breed, who was to act as hunter and purveyor to the party.

Having premised this much for the sake of an intelligible narrative, I will merely state—passing over all that occurred in the interim—that on or about the middle of July, we came in sight of the Rock of Independence, an immense mass of granite rising out of the level prairie like huge battlemented castle, surrounded by a wild waste of sterile desolation.

This singular rock is composed of red granite, covering an area of probably three acres and rising to a height of about two hundred feet, entirely destitute of herbage, and can be seen at the distance of at least a hundred miles, in approaching from the East. We encamped at its base, and found it literally covered over with names and inscriptions. Few travellers pass this way, I presume, without adding their names as slight memorials, to show passerby that here–desolate and solitary as the place may well be considered–restless white men have been before them, in the same wild chase after change and excitement. We ascended to the summit of this rock, and the scene that burst upon our astonished sight might well have recompensed us for a far more difficult and tedious undertaking.

As far as the eye could reach, with an uninterrupted horizon on every side, the field of vision was literally covered and blackened over with multitudinous herds of buffaloes. I had heard, or read of such things; but here was the reality, far exceeding in its naked truth the romantic exaggeration of the novelist, or the fanciful embellishments of the poet. It was a sight never to be forgotten.

It was quickly determined to have some sport; and in the space of a very few minutes every man in camp who owned, or thought he owned a good horse or mule, was mounted upon his back, determined to try his luck in a neck-or-nothing chase after those shaggy denizens of the western wilds. Determined to let no feature of the prairie life escape my experience, and having as fleet an animal as any in camp, with the exception, perhaps of a powerful gray horse that Captain Stewart rode, I was amongst the first to leap into the saddle. We proceeded leisurely towards the countless herds in compact order, led on by Captain Stewart and Antione Clemment, his half-breed hunter, with a few men bringing up the rear, with led mules having empty pack-saddles on their backs, in order to take into camp the anticipated spoils of the hunt.

Three Years in the Rocky Mountains

Having approached within three or four hundred yards of this dense mass of animal life, on a preconcerted signal being given by Capt. Stewart, each man put spurs to his horse, and at utmost speed we dashed upon the traces of the already flying bisons. From this moment my recollections are altogether personal. The scurry and rapidity of my horse's movements precluded the possibility of my observing the motions of my companions. On arousing from the sudden and dreamlike stupor, with sudden and rapid motion on horseback rarely fails to engender, I found myself in the center of a living cataract, almost blinded by the stream of sand and gravel thrown in my face from the hoofs of the terrified mass in the desperate and headlong flight. A cataract, it might well be called, for we were descending into an immense hollow or ravine, which had been hidden from our eyes by the apparent levelness of the whole surface of the prairie, at an angle of little less than thirty degrees. The excitement was great in proportion to the danger, which indeed now appeared to be imminent. As yet I had not fired a shot. The gigantic animals, snorting with terror and foaming with fatigue, were literally pressing against my horse on every side. Their bloodshot eyes, gleaming fitfully from under the penthouse of their bushy eye-brows, and their shaggy manes, streaming meteor-like on the swift and cleaving air, was a sight at once sublime, fearful, and menacing. To have checked my horse at this time would have been in all probability to incur instant death, as the masses behind would certainly have trodden me, horse and all, into jelly, I did what was much safer and more reasonable in the premises. I fired into an immense bull that pressed heavily against my right stirrup, and as the muzzle of my rifle touched its ribs, its report was immediately followed by the fall of the huge animal, which rolled headlong on the ground.

The effect of this shot was electrical. The herd which before had borne and pressed upon my horse to a very alarming degree, now divided and burst away on every side, as if a volcano had suddenly risen in their midst. Now that I could check my horse with safety, I pulled up, in order to contemplate at leisure the mighty animal that I had so suddenly, and as it now appeared to me when the hurry and excitement were over, needlessly, deprived of life. The enormous creature lay prostrate on the ground, with its head twisted partly under its bulk, its only visible eye white and glazed. The ball had done its mission at once. I cannot say that I experienced any of those feelings of exultation usually considered the portion and meed of a hunter contemplating the victim of his successful exertions. Its death was wholly gratuitous, as even its flesh could not be used, being at that season of the year excessively strong and rank.

After making my way out of the ravine, in which I found myself on killing the buffalo, I looked around in order to ascertain my position with regard to the camp. I found I had ridden many miles in the headlong chase; for though but little past mid-day when it began, the slanting rays of the evening sun were playing in dazzling brilliancy upon the come-like and blood-read summit of the Rock of Independence, which stood far away in the southern horizon. But the day's sport was not doomed to conclude without further and still more perilous excitement.

Hearing the report of the fire arms to the right, I rode rapidly in that direction. The shots came in quick succession, mingled with the wild yells and shouts, which made me almost instinctively look to the priming of my rifle and holster pistols as the thought of Indians rushed upon my alarmed fancy. Emerging from a deep hollow that had concealed them from my view, appeared in rapid succession Capt. Stewart, Antoine Clemment, the hunter, and five or six others of the party, in apparently hot and furious pursuit of some deadly enemy. Putting my spurs to my spirited and active mare, I was soon up with the foremost of the chase, and just in time to witness its successful termination. An immense grizzly bear, desperate from fatigue and furious with pain and terror, for he was badly wounded, his muzzle and skin being dabbled with blood, now stood at bay, determined, as it appeared, to retreat no further, but to sell his life as dearly as possible where he stood. The coup-de-grace was given to this fierce monster by Capt. Stewart, from the muzzle of a holster pistol, which pierced the brain of this ferocious sultan of the western deserts, and lain him life-less on the prarie-sward. He was quickly denuded of his skin, by the half-breed, Clemment, which, along with some portions of his fat, was transferred to the back of a pack-mule, already well loaded with buffalo meat, but not before furious resistance had been made by some other animals upon whose backs it had been first attempted to place this, to them, unwelcome trophy, for the scent of this creature strikes with deadly terror every animal subjected to its influence.

When we arrived in camp, the shades of light had long since settled on the landscape, and the joyful shouts that welcomed our return plainly revealed that considerable apprehension had been entertained for our safety.

Having eaten a hearty supper of roasted buffalo meat, basted and seasoned with the fat of the bear, many a thrilling story of 'perilous adventure' and 'hair-breadth' having been told in the intervals, worn out and jaded with fatigue and excitement of the day, I retired to rest, with my saddle for a pillow, and the green sward for a bed, the star-lit and eternal vault, for a canopy, and for a lullaby the melancholy howlings of innumerable wolves, which, however, neither retarded nor broke the serenity of the slumbers.

To one who has been worn down by sickness, and a consequent prey to bodily languor, and an apathetic listlessness and dullness of all mental powers, how delightful it is to wake, as if from a troubled and feverish sleep, in the full enjoyment of health—to the vivid and ever-varying feelings and incidents of a prairie tour!

The atmosphere fresh and exhilarating; the 'brave o'erhanging canopy' deeply and darkly beautiful, with here and there a stray cloud floating over its azure depths, to break the uniformity of its gladdening undulating country, stretching far, far away, in its rich and variegated luxuriance, creating in my mind, along with an overpowering sense of delight, a vague and indistinct feeling compounded of mystery and awe, at the thoughts of what may lie beyond; these, and a thousand sights and sounds beside conspire to give to prairie life an enthralling fascination, that clings to the mind forever after. I therefore do not wonder at the fact which has come under my own observations, that individuals, who having once tasted the sweets of this roving and adventurous life, on returning to the haunts of civilization, and of law-abiding people, have languished and pined after those irresponsible solitude where man is amendable to neither laws nor social restrictions, but revels in the untrammeled liberty, of a fierce and all but animal existence.

The country, on a near approach to the Rocky Mountains, is, for the most part, singularly wild and uninviting in its aspect. It is, indeed, relieved in many instances, by the traveller's falling, as it were, upon fairy nooks of surpassing beauty and verdure. The general character of the existing scenery is anything but attractive. Immense plains, covered over with a thick growth of wormwood and other unsightly shrubs, fatigue the eyes with monotony. The sight of a herd of wild horses, of buffaloes, or of antelopes, or perhaps of elk or black-tailed deer, is not an unfrequent interruption of the solitude of the scene. Vast piles of naked rocks are scattered at frequent intervals over the face of the landscape, lending, by their ruggedness, an additional wildness, and a more intense desolation to the aspect of nature.

On the thirtieth of July 1836, towards evening we came in sight of Wind River Mountains. This is one of the loftiest of the chain; and, as it loomed up vast and distinct on our northwestern horizon, encompassed by a blue and gauze-like atmosphere, with the rays of the level sun burnishing with indescribable splendor the eternal snows that rested on its summit, we involuntarily checked our horses to gaze at leisure upon this august and magnificent spectacle.

To those who, reared in the cities or plains, have never beheld the grander manifestations of the invisible Omnipotence; whose calm and abiding consciousness has slept untroubled by the entrance of one all-absorbing and overmastering emotion; to such, the first view of a huge mountain become an epoch, from which are dated their mind's subsequent annals.

Three Years in the Rocky Mountains

The soul has received a "new sense," as it is aptly expressed by Byron in his grandest of poems, Manfred; the portals of the inner man have been thrown majestically back, and a fresh and welcome guest has entered to abide there evermore. For myself, I had tried life in a variety of aspects. Every chord in the mental organism had been touched. Bitter experience and deadly trial, senseless passion, and still more senseless weakness, distant travel and constant vicissitude, on the ocean and in the desert—all of those had been my portion. But even these had not so "filed" my mind, but that the presence, though far off, of this giant peak, which soared in haughty grandeur through the evening sky, so luminous and yet so cold, impressed it with a grateful sense of the goodness and power of that being, whose dwelling place is in the "Empire of Eternity."

Several days passed over, when rose to view the continuous links of that vast chain of mountains, which, running almost due north and south, forms the dividing ridge between those immense plains, through whose ample bosoms the great rivers of the northern majority of this continent take their devious and sparkling course, to empty themselves into the two cardinal oceans of the globe—the Atlantic and Pacific.

Two more days passed, and we entered the great Shoshonee, or Snake Valley. On either side of the pass, the mountains rise to a great height, with jagged saw-like summits. The air was fresh and bracing, and the innumerable flowers which our horses trampled upon at every step, sent forth a delicious fragrance.

This valley has an average width of about three miles and is the great opening from this side of the territory of Oregon.

Here we were joined by some of the trappers and hunters from the general rendezvous of the banks of the Cis-ke-dee, or Green River. They had been made aware of our near approach by one of our men, who had started on ahead as an "Express" shortly after we had crossed the north fork of the Platte; and they had come to escort and welcome us into camp.

Three Years in the Rocky Mountains

We came very near mistaking them for Indians; for, being dressed in every respect like the aborigines of the country, and from imitating them likewise in their savage yells and furious riding, it was well that our temporary error led us to no serious consequences. Here was a tremendous shaking of hands, firing off of guns, and asking of questions, and all so confused and huddled together, that it was utterly impossible either to understand, or to be understood in turn. By and by, however, the tumult subsided; and as we rode along, we conversed upon such subjects as were uppermost in our respective minds—we, enquiring anxiously about the sort of life led by the trappers, what were its dangers, and what its enjoyments; and they in their turn, eagerly asking after all that had occurred in the United States, which they invariably called "the settlements," since they had left it, perhaps several years previous. As these were tolerably comprehensive questions on either side, it may be readily supposed that they were not very speedily or easily exhausted.

In the course of a few hours' gentle riding, we were made aware of our near proximity to the trappers' encampment; for in turning a sharp angle of the valley, we came suddenly upon a long line of beautiful Indian tents, arranged in regular order, and stretching away for at least two miles in perspective, and terminating in a wide and circular array of the same romantic and fairy-looking dwellings.

As I gazed in rapt, admiration upon this, to me, dream-like exhibition, my mind instantly reverted to the storied wonders of my childhood and early youth, and I almost expected every moment to see issuing from the bosom of this Indian cantonment, in martial pomp and pride, the mailed and steel-clad forms of the old feudal times, so striking was its resemblance to the pictures already enshrined in my imagination from the pouring over the delightful pages of Scott and Froissart, whose inimitable descriptions floated before my mental eye in all the gorgeous splendor of the encampments of Agincourt and Cressy, of the Lion Hearted Richard and Saladin, and of the magnificent tournament of Ashby-de-la-Zouch.

Three Years in the Rocky Mountains

Neither was there an absence of other accessories to complete a fancied resemblance. The tents were identical in shape with those we see represented in old English engravings as belonging to knights and warriors; and between and around their dazzling white and symmetrical outlines, were grouped in exquisite tableaux the dusky Apollo-shaped forms of the flower of Indian chivalry.

The first row of 'lodges' was occupied by a large party of Crow Indians, who had been attracted thither by the presence of American Fur Company's hunters, with whom they are always anxious to keep up at least the appearance of friendship, and likewise to exchange their simple wares, such as buffalo robes and dressed deer and antelope skins, for other commodities, guns, ammunition, blankets, tobacco, beads and like-articles which they and the trappers barter to their mutual satisfaction.

And now having joined the great and general rendezvous of the hunters and trappers from many a different scene of mountain and valley, secluded stream and mystic glen, and having undergone the initiatory process of asking and being asked a thousand questions, and turning on every side to find nothing but unbounded hospitality and solicitous good will, let me pause one moment to invoke the aid of some kindly sprite, to vouch safe to one rainbow ray of genial inspiration, whilst I attempt to sketch scenes and incidents to which nothing short of genius of a Scott, Cervantes or Le Sage could do aught like adequate justice.

On the second evening after our arrival at the general rendezvous, I attended an entertainment given by Capt. Stewart to the mountain trappers, and as I had an excellent opportunity of observing the lights and shadows of these men's characters, brought out in bold and strong relief, I shall endeavor to sketch a few of the most prominent among them, trusting to the current of my narrative to develop more at large, the various peculiarities of their histories and dispositions, as exhibited in connection with circumstances where not a few of them acted daring and extraordinary parts.

Three Years in the Rocky Mountains

The entertainment alluded to, was given by the English Captain in a large tent, which he had occasionally used in his journey up from the 'States,' and which resembled very much in size and general construction those now used in the U.S. Army by general and field officers on a campaign, and was capable of containing, with perfect comfort to themselves, some twenty-five or thirty persons. On the present occasion it contained some thirty men in all. Most of these were noted characters in the mountains; and some of them, if drawn to the life by the graphic pens of a Scott or a Cooper, would not fail to rank with the best delineations of those inimitable writers.

To an ample supply of fresh buffalo meat, the captain had added to his hospital board (which board, be it understood, was neither more nor less than the hard ground, and not altogether bare either, but covered over with the most verdant and thick carpeting of grass) some choice old liquors of his own importation, to which, in the course of the repast, ample justice was done; and if the quantity swallowed be any criterion by which to judge the quality of any given drinkables, then were the Captain's superlative indeed.

On the right of Captain Stewart, sat, or rather squatted in oriental fashion, one of the most remarkable men of this remarkable assemblage. This was Mr. James Bridger, or "Jim" Bridger, as he was always termed, who had come to that country in the first instance, in the employment of Gen. Ashley, and after having acted for a series of years as a caterer of hunter for that gentlemen's mess was finally engaged, after a shifting and turning of the dam fortune's wheel, by the North American Fur Company, to fill the difficult and hazardous position he now held as a partisan or leader of beaver hunting parties; for which he was admirably adapted, from his wide and thorough acquaintance with the whole mountain regions from the Russian settlements to the Californias, and of every nook and hidden lake and unfrequented stream where these singularly shy and sagacious animals 'most do congregate.' Bridger had likewise, in addition to the above mentioned qualifications, other qualifications, other qualities of scarcely less importance, and without which the former would have been comparatively little value. These were a complete and absolute understanding of the Indian character in all its different phases, and a firm, though by no means over cautious, distrust with regard to these savages, based upon his own large experience of their general perfidy, cunning and atrocity. To sum up, his bravery was unquestionable, his horsemanship equally so, and as to his skill with the rifle, it will scarcely be doubted, when we mention the fact that he had been known to kill twenty buffaloes by the same number of consecutive shots. The physical conformation of this man was in admirable keeping with his character. Tall–six feet at least–muscular, without an ounce of superfluous flesh to impede its force or exhaust its elasticity, he might have served as a model for a sculptor or a painter, by which to express the perfection of graceful strength and easy activity. One remarkable feature of this man I had almost omitted, and that was his neck, which rivalled his head in size and thickness, and which gave the upper portion of his otherwise well-formed person a somewhat outre and unpleasant appearance. His cheek bones were high, his nose hooked or aquiline, the expression of his eyes mild and thoughtful, and that of his face grave almost to solemnity. To complete the picture, he was perfectly ignorant of all knowledge contained in books, not even knowing the letters of the alphabet; put perfect faith in dreams or omen, and was unutterably scandalized if even the most childish of the superstitions of the Indian were treated with anything like contempt or disrespect; for in all these he was a firm and devout believer.

Next to Bridger, sat Bill Williams, the Nestor of the trappers. A more heterogeneous compound than this man, it has never been my fortune to meet withal. He was confessedly the best trapper in the mountains; could catch more beaver, and kill more horses by hard riding, in so doing, than any that had ever set a trap in these waters. He could likewise drink more liquor, venture father alone in the eager pursuit of game into the neighborhood of dangerous and hostile Indians, spend more money, and spend it quicker than any other man. He could likewise swear harder, and longer, and coin more queer and awful oaths than any pirate that ever blasphemed under a black flag, over a black ship, and from a blacker heart. He could shoot (so he said) higher and deeper, wider and closer, straighter and crookeder, and more rounding, and more every way, than "ever a son of a–of them all," as I had the ineffable pleasure of hearing him say myself, the very next morning after the English Captain's hospitable entertainment; and which very word he made use (or abuse) of in daring the whole camp, the world included, to a proof of skill with him in shooting at a mark. This astonishing personage was near seventy year of age.

On the opposite side of the table, or whatever the reader may choose to call that portion of greed sward that served as such, was placed one Joe Meek, or "Major" Meek, as he was rather indifferently called–another curious instance of unique character, as is so frequently associations, are different from those of the rest of mankind. Meek's real history and adventures, if fairly and honestly written out, would be a book to make the fortune of its author.

Three Years in the Rocky Mountains

In juxtaposition with the last describes personage, sat, or rather reclined, one to whom I would call the reader's particular attention. This man's name was Head. It would take a stronger pencil than the author of these sketches is capable of wielding, to embody the dark depths and shadows that alone could make up a true picture of this ruthless and remorseless original. The circumstances about to be related, will place his character in a clearer and more intelligible light, than could any amount of description, however carefully or elaborately composed.

Some two or three years previous to this time, Capt. Stewart, (now Sir William) had arrived at the headquarters of rendezvous of the Fur Company from the United State, on one of his periodical excursions to this part of the world, and brought in his train, as a servant or waiter, an Indian half-breed, a Creole of St. Charles, Missouri, and whose tragic fate is the subject of the following brief narrative.

This man was an excellent hunter, and we frequently employed as such by Capt. Stewart, and was, we believe, taken altogether, considered a very fair specimen of this class of men, who are not famous for either honesty or other essentials of good character. One day he was missed, as likewise to of Capt. Stewart's best saddle horses, and it was immediately suspected that he had stolen them and gone over to join the Hudson Bay Company, at one of their posts on the upper part of the Columbia. These facts and surmises were mentioned to Captain Stewart, who being naturally indignant at such and ungrateful and unworthy treatment, from one whom he had always treated with frank and considerate kindness, remarked, in the heat and passion of the moment—words that he would afterwards have given his whole fortune to recall—that he would give any one in camp five hundred dollars for his scalp, with or without the horses. These unfortunate words, with the attending circumstances, were quickly circulated through the encampment, and having formed the talk of the hour, were dismissed, to make way for other subject of fresher and more engrossing interest. But there was one man upon whose mind they had fallen, and like the spear of Ithuriel, had changed a hateful and contemptible object into a hideous and portentous field. This was Mark Head, who, it was afterwards remembered, was seen to saddle his horse and ride out of camp with his rifle and other equipments, as if going to hunt buffalo, and no particular notice was taken of it at the time, as such were matters of daily and hourly occurrence.

The evening closed upon the day without anything having taken place to mar or interrupt the usual pastime and diversion of the camp. Morning rose fresh and lovely as is her wont in these eternal solitudes. The events of yesterday were hardly remembered, and the hour of noon was fast approaching when the slumberous stillness of the camp was rudely broken by the rapid trampling of horses' feet, and furious and frantic yells that appeared to issue from a cloud of dust that came borne across the prairie upon the summer breeze in the direction of the tents. This cleared away; and now it was seen to be a solitary horsemen, and that horseman was soon recognized to be Mark Head; and still onward he came, shouting and yelling like one under demoniacal possession, which he doubtless was; and holding aloft on the muzzle of his rifle something that looked like black and glossy, but which no one could yet recognize. Nearer and nearer still he came, thundering on, and grinding the solid earth beneath his horse's feet into an impalpable powder, that floated away like the foaming waves in a vessel's wake; and now he is upon them, and past them, checking his horse strongly and suddenly in front of Capt. Stewart's tent, leaps from his back, and holds up exultingly to view the dissevered and blood-dripping scalp of Charles the Creole! Had the Avenger of Blood stood before him, greater could not have been the blank horror and consternation of Capt. Stewart, than on witnessing this direful apparition. The few hasty and unpremeditated words he had so unhappily spoken, had passed from his mind almost as soon as uttered; but here they were recalled to him in fiery and terrific distinctness by the ruthless wretch who stood before him, boldly claiming the proffered reward for this deliberate murder.

Three Years in the Rocky Mountains

In the excitement of the moment, many talked of executing summary justice upon Head; and the wretched man had to consult his safety by absenting himself several weeks from the society and companionship of his brother hunters. But in a very short time, this tragical occurrence ceased to be talked about, and gradually lapsed from the minds of all, as other events usurped the interest it had for a season inspired.

Head himself, afterwards related the manner in which he killed the Creole, and which was simply as follows: On leaving the encampment, he had observed the trail made by the horses which the missing man had taken with him in his flight, and following it up all that day, had come upon him in the evening about sunset, and just as he was in the act of cutting up a buffalo that he appeared to have lately killed. The ill-gated man was somewhat startled at first, but Head quickly re-assured him by his frankness and cordiality. He even applauded his act of carrying off Capt. Stewart's horses. The Creole's suspicions having been thus completely disarmed, he naturally relapsed into his occupation of butchering, in which he had been interrupted by Head, when the latter, seizing his opportunity, shot his unsuspecting victim through the heart, and after having scalped him, returned to camp in the manner above described.

The first few days after our arrival at the rendezvous, were one continued scene of wild revelry and excitement. A quantity of liquor which we had brought along with us in order to give hunters what is termed a good spree, was the immediate cause of this state of things.

It has always been the custom of the American Fur Company to supply the persons of its employment, once a year, with a large amount of this pernicious stimulant; induced thereto, no doubt, by a knowledge that in the thoughtless and extravagant exhilaration, many of their best and most industrious trappers are led to squander in a few short days the hard earned wages of the whole years of almost incessant labor, danger and privation. It was really pitiable to see some of these poor fellows on recovering from a paroxism of frantic and self-induced madness, in which they had spent everything coming to them on the books of the company, to the amount very often of several hundred dollars, and on the possession of which they perhaps had built their calculations of retiring from this wild and hazardous life, to the peaceful occupations of civilized society. In thus encouraging and furnishing the means of intoxication, it is not going too far to say, that many of these men have felt themselves defrauded and cheated out of their money by the company, whose interest it was to keep them in the country, and which is especially anxious to retain in its service, all such as are due a large sum, as the risk of life is very great—from the hand of villainous Indians—and from a thousand unforseen casualties that threaten the hunter on every side. In case of death the Company becomes executor to the deceased, and in general they appear to have been poorly rewarded for their trouble and exertions. I know not how it is, but every man who has died in that country for the last twenty years, died in its debt, and many persons who the day and the hour preceding their death, were thought to have a large sum due them on the books of the Company, have yet been found, incredible as it may appear, to have not only worth nothing, but a few dollars less than even that.

But the pecuniary loss is by no means the only or worse consequence of supplying these men with intoxicating liquors. Scenes of bloodshed and violence are by no means of unfrequent occurrence. An incident which happened at this time will forcibly illustrate the tenor of these remarks.

Two individuals of the Company named Carson and Shunar, the former native of Missouri, and the latter a French Creole of Lower Canada, had long been considered the best men respectively of what were termed the French and American portions of the camp. A feeling of rivalry had long existed between these two parties, which was however generally harmless, except the demon of alcohol were present, to fan into flames the embers of their slumbering animosities. Such was the case on the present occasion.

Three Years in the Rocky Mountains

Shunar mounted upon his horse–rifle in hand paraded through the camp, breathing defiance in no measured terms, and daring any American to meet him in open fight. For a long time no one seemed inclined to have anything to do with this formidable bully; who thinking that this state of things was the result of intimidation, fearing that the honor of the American trappers would be compromised by allowing the Canadian to proceed unopposed, Carson seized a loaded piece, and proceeding outside the encampment to the place where the horses were grazing, deliberately bridled his animal, and riding into camp, shouted aloud to Shunar 'to look out for himself, as he intended to give him the contents of his piece.' They rode toward each other at full speed, and each delivered his fire in passing at the same instant. The result was, that Carson was uninjured, the ball of his antagonist passing through the hair of his head, whilst Shunar's right hand was shattered severely, and the thumb carried entirely away.

A desperate fight, or rather a massacre which took place a few days afterwards, more than realized my previous conceptions of the reckless indifference to human life, which becomes a mental habitude of those who are constantly exposed to situations of great insecurity and danger.

I think I have mentioned in former sketch, that a large number of Indians, of different tribes were assembled at our rendezvous. There were about five thousand encamped around us, to which our eighty or a hundred tents seemed but as a core or nucleus to the large surrounding mass. Of these the largest party was of Snakes of Shoshonees–in the centre of whose country we then were, –likewise a large party of Crows, a considerable number of Nes Percies and Flat Heads, and lastly a band of some three or four hundred Pawnarks. These last mentioned were encamped at about a mile and a half's distance, on the margin of the Green River.

It appears that in the raids and forays which Indians are constantly in the habit of making into the nations and territories of each other, for the purpose principally of stealing horses, and also of getting as many of the scalps of their enemies as they can conveniently secure without incurring any very heroic extent of danger–the Pawnarks had stolen a very fine stallion belonging to the principal chief of the Flat Heads. These last on coming into the immediate neighborhood of heir wiley foes, had recognized the missing animal, and having slyly recaptured him, had him now in their own rightful possession.

A Pawnark chief impudently demanded the restoration of the brute as belonging to the tribe. This was denied on the part of the Flat Heads, and the horse was finally given into the hands of Bridger for security and safe keeping. As this person was leading off the disputed property, the Pawnark chief stepped resolutely forward and attempted to wrest the halter from his hand, by which the horse was confined, when a scuffle ensued, in which Bridger's rifle was either intentionally or accidentally discharged. This served as the signal for a general onslaught. The hunters and trappers who had gathered around at the commencement of the difficulty, from motives of curiosity, now poured in a murderous fire upon the surprised and astonished Pawnarks, who had been calmly awaiting on horseback the result of their chief's interference. Nine saddles were immediately emptied of their occupants, and probably as many more men were mortally wounded, but who were able to retain their seats and escape, that peculiar, and most wonderful tenacity of life, which has been observed to belong to the physical constitution of the Indian, and which many times enables him to survive wounds and injuries which would prove instantly fatal to the more delicate organization of the white man. To catch horses and pursue the Indians was with our men the work of a few moments, but as the former had the start, they all succeeded in regaining their camp in safety, whither they had no sooner arrived than they threw up temporary breastworks of brush and sapplings, so effectually to protect them from the balls of their adversaries. The poor wretches who had fallen in the commencement of the affray were tomahawked and scalped on the spot, and their disfigured and mutilated remains were dragged about a mile from the encampment, and there left to be devoured by the wolf, and his hideous companion, the California vulture.

That these proceedings were—to use the rawest terms—harsh and unjustifiable on the part of the whites, admits of neither doubt nor denial. The only palliation they admit of, is to be found in the following consideration:

That these Indians were never known to be friendly to the whites, and were moreover vehemently suspected of having secretly murdered many of the trappers, whose mangled bodies had frequently been found in the vicinity of their haunts, and those deaths could in nowise be accounted for, but by supposing them to be the guilty authors. And secondly that the Flat Heads were and ever had been the consistent and undeviating friends of the "pale faces," and that they were the only tribe in the mountains who could say with firm and unsuspected truth, "that the blood of the white man had never left its black stain on their badges." These suggestions will in some measure explain, why the trappers espoused with such eagerness the cause of their faithful

Indian allies when these allies were subjected to insult and maltreatment by a more powerful tribe, and why what at first sight appears to have been an act of wanton and destructive cruelty, was but the conflagration lit up by the long smouldering sparks, in which the whites, canceled and balanced up, a protracted and long deferred arrearage of vengeance.

The following day the Pawnarks disappeared from our neighborhood, and our men, congratulated themselves on the consideration, that in future they would have to deal with open and acknowledge foes, where before they were subjected to the treacherous wiles of professed friends, but in reality secret and deadly enemies.

About this time the gaiety of our camp was greatly increased by the arrival of the Hudson Bay Company from Fort Vancouver on the lower Columbia. They encamped about two miles apart from us, on a beautiful meadow, surrounded by willows, on an elbow of the Cis-ke-dee. A constant and most cordial intercourse was kept up from this time, until the conclusion of the Rendezvous; and I can safely say that some of the most pleasant hours I have ever passed, were spent in the hospital marquee of Mr. McLeod, the principal superintendent of the British Company in this part of the world. His coadjutors were Mr. McLean and Mr. McKay, the latter gentleman the son by a Kanacka woman, of that McKay so frequently spoken of in Washington Irving's Astoria, as a daring and resolute adventurer. The son, if the universal rumor might be believed, was not a whit behind the father, in determined and reckless courage, as many Indian tribe could bear ample though unwilling testimony.

Great was the sport of the members of the two Companies in getting up races and in testing the speed of their respective horses, but in the long run the victories were balanced, neither having much to boast of in the way of success. But the period of our sojourn together was fast drawing to a close. Already had the Hudson Bay Company taken its departure. Already had one or two small parties of independent trappers set forth on their isolated and precarious occupation, trusting in mutual firmness and intrepidity of each other, to clear the way in every emergency of difficulty and danger.

The "Booshways," as the managers of the North American Fur Company are technically termed the mountaineers, had for some days been silently arranging their plans for the next twelve month's campaign against the beaver and otter, and in selecting a Rendezvous for the coming year, and likewise in distributing the men into parties, under their different leaders. Now all was completed, and we only waited the signals to disperse for our various hunting grounds. One party was to proceed to the Quiaterre country, on the confines of north-western Mexico and California; another was to hunt the "old Park," a large portion of territory, embracing the sources of the Columbia, the Missouri and the Platte, and a great many of their tributary streams.

The party to which I attached myself was the largest, it having the most dangerous country to trap in, its range extending through the Crows and Blackfeet, and from this crossing the great chain of mountains into the Oregon territory, and numbering in all about seventy-five or eighty men.

I will here close this "Sketch" with a brief narration of a disastrous event that befell Mr. Gray, a missionary from among the tribes at the north Columbia.

This gentleman had travelled up from the Pacific under the escort of the Hudson Bay Company, for the purpose of joining the American Fur Company's camp, and of proceeding down the returning of that body, to the United States. He had in his charge, six young men of the Chinook tribe of Indians, whom it was his intention to have educated by the "Board of Missions," and of taking them back after this had been accomplished, to aid and assist in the pious and philanthropic object of instructing and their own and neighboring tribes. This was no doubt an excellent idea, and unquestionably, under better auspices, have been productive of highly beneficial consequences. But how melancholy and deplorable was the result!

Mr. Gray, contrary to all advice, and to every consideration urgently laid before him by the most experienced men, persisted in his purpose of proceeding alone on his route to the States without awaiting for the escort and protection of the Company. The result of this course was precisely what had been anticipated. He had not proceeded above ten days' journey—and the wonder was that he suffered to go thus far— when he was surrounded by a large band of the upper Sioux, who, after having made him and one other white man he had in his little party stand to one side, they deliberately murdered before his eyes, the poor Indians, whom, by the wanton absurdity and wrong-headedness of his conduct, he had thus consigned to an untimely fate.

Mr. Gray and the other man were allowed to escape with their lives, but their horses and every particle of baggage was taken from them, and they were compelled to shift for themselves the best was they could on the open prairie, with the prospect of starvation on one hand, and great danger and unspeakable fatigue on the other. In this forlorn and hopeless condition, they were providentially permitted to arrive at Fort Laramie, on the north fork of the Platte, but in a situation so woe-begone and miserable as to strike with horror its warm hearted and hospitable occupants.

There is no doubt that Mr. Gray was betrayed into this course by a senseless and over weening reliance on the special protection of divine providence. But the Bible, and common sense if not the Bible, should have taught him, that presumptuous confidence is alien to the true gospel spirit, and that even the Christian is nowhere promised an exemption from the ordinary consequences of rashness and imprudence—and that to think and act otherwise, is in effect to suppose, that God is to do everything, and man nothing.

Bridger's remark to Mr. Gray, when the latter was about to set out on his ill-omened expedition, struck me forcibly at the time. It was in answer to some of the other's foolish and fantastic dogmas. "Sir," said the old hunter, slapping his right hand heavily on the breach of his rifle, "the grace of God won't carry a man through these prairies! It takes powder and ball."

Three Years in the Rocky Mountains